Languid Lusciousness with Lemon

poems by

Joan Leotta

Finishing Line Press
Georgetown, Kentucky

Languid Lusciousness with Lemon

Copyright © 2017 by Joan Leotta
ISBN 978-1-63534-145-4 First Edition
All rights reserved under International and Pan-American Copyright Conventions.
No part of this book may be reproduced in any manner whatsoever without written permission from the publisher, except in the case of brief quotations embodied in critical articles and reviews.

ACKNOWLEDGMENTS

Languid Lusciousness with Lemon…..*Silver Birch*, October 2015 in it's My Sweet Word Series
Apples at Nonna's…. first in *Poet's Domain*, Volume Four, 1991
Back Porch Morning,…..,*A Quiet Courage*, April 2015
Sampling Oysters….. *Postcard Poems and Prose*, Spring 2015
Around the Round Oak Table…..*Fragrance Magazine*, Spring 2014
Fourth of July Picnic, 1955…..*Righter Monthly*, July 2015
Al Dente…..*Poeming Pigeons Anthology on Food*, 2015
The Conversation… *New Press Literary Quarterly*, 1996
Dreaming Across the Styx… *Red Wolf Journal*, Fall 2014
The Queen of Long Division…..*Silver Birch*, October 2015, Halloween Series
A Platter of Mezze ….. *Inspiration of the Heart*, March 21 2015; Melinda Cochrane website http://www.mciwritershouse.com/authors-spotlight

Publisher: Leah Maines

Editor: Christen Kincaid

Cover Art: Joan Leotta

Author Photo: Brenda Kokenos, www.brenkostudio.com

Cover Design: Elizabeth Maines McCleavy

Printed in the USA on acid-free paper.
Order online: www.finishinglinepress.com
         also available on amazon.com

               Author inquiries and mail orders:
                     Finishing Line Press
                       P. O. Box 1626
               Georgetown, Kentucky 40324
                         U. S. A.

Table of Contents

Languid Lusciousness with Lemon 1
Apples at Nonna's 2
Back Porch Morning 3
Sampling Oysters 4
Kitty Hawk Hang Glider School 5
On the Making of Pizzelle 7
Around the Round Oak Table 9
Strawberries 10
Peach Vendor 11
Peaches and Dares 13
Two Cups of Coffee 14
Turkish Delight 15
In Rhapsodic Praise of Biscuits 17
Fourth of July Picnic 1955 18
The Queen of Long Division 19
Al Dente 21
The Conversation 22
Dreaming Across the Styx 23
A Platter of Mezze 25

Languid Lusciousness with Lemon is a collection of poems about food and family. I dedicate it to my family, the people with whom I share daily, at the dinner table, the joys and sorrows of life.

Languid Lusciousness with Lemon

Languid lusciousness
lines the tables at the peach vendor's
farmers' market stall.
Rich with juice, the red
peaches wait
on the side
to be sliced,
imparting Eliot's
immortality
with each bite.
Yet, my cook's instinct
notes those slices will need
a squeeze of lemon
to retain their color
when I fan them out
on the dessert plate.
Life's sweetness stands out,
oft best preserved
when accented with tart.

Apples at Nonna's

We don't buy the apples piled in
10-for-a dollar bags
in the supermarket in our city.
We drive forever to the
crisp blue skies of autumn in
      "upstate" New York
where apples answer to many names.

Nonna fills the table with plates of
   Dad's favorite things,
     and a bowl of chocolates for me and
     we all talk until bedtime.
In the morning we must decide where and what to pick.
Nonna begins the litany of the apples:
       "The Lattios have the best Pound Sweets and Macintosh."
"Can we go there, Dad? "
Dad just smiles.
       "Campbell's has the best Number Tens and Northern Spy."
"Can we go *there*, Dad?"
Dad just smiles.
       "The Rivelli Orchard has top Macombs."
"Can we go *there*, Dad?"

Dad stirs his coffee one more time, then drains the cup.
Nonna asks, "Where are you going?"
Dad smiles. "Campbell's—like always."
Nonna hugs me as I put on my coat:
    "*Ti piace la raccolta delle mele?*"
So many words for apples—
     Number tens, Macombs, Delicious Gold and Red,
     Pound Sweets, Northern Spy, Staymans,
     MacIntonsh, *Mele.*

Apples taste better when you know them by name.

Back Porch Morning

Brick pillars defined its limits.
Square, small, docked
like a small lifeboat
trailing behind her ship of a home
in the vast green sea of her lawn.

Grandma and I ate our
buttered toast without crusts
sitting at a steel
cafe table.

Afterwards, she
stood on the top step—
tossed crumbs and crusts
onto that green sea of a lawn.

"Come!" she called.
Every sparrow in the world
descended.
My grandma
could summon birds
from an empty sky!

One morning
curiosity trumped awe.
"How do they hear you?"

Smiling, she answered,
"Everyone hears
when called to table."

Sampling Oysters

My daughter and I picked an
auspicious week, then trekked north
to Prince Edward Island
for a bivalve extravaganza.
Together we slurped bivalves
tasting of bays and of ocean—
Malpeque, Raspberry Point and more.
Some briny; others sweet.
Jennie recorded the nuances,
savored each oyster's unique flavor.
I savored the found pearl
of our togetherness.

Kitty Hawk Hang Glider School

The glider school brochure
promised an adventure—
Da Vinci design
joined with Icarus' spirit.
Such was the only recompense
we could offer our teenage son
when he traded time with friends
for time with parents
during senior year spring break.
Beach time, but with parents.

Out on Kitty Hawk's dunes at last,
At the top of the highest one.
as his instructor watched,
Joe lay flat,
strapped into harness.

At the signal,
Joe began the course
plodding, then running
down that dune
building to flight speed.

Finally, glider's ungainly array of metal, canvas and Joe
caught a stray air current
whipping through the dunes.

Snatched up, Joe was above the sand!

As I watched, he hovered
between the earth and its shadow
skimming over the sand
in his own small, low, bit of sky.

Airborne, though not yet soaring, he was indeed, flying, even if for just a moment.

All alone.
Not Wilbur. Not Orville.
Just Joe.
A solo flight.
The first of many yet to come.

On the Making of Pizzelle

"Please write your recipe for *pizzelle*,"
I demanded one winter afternoon,
"They are my favorite cookie."

"They are a lot of work,"
Mom warned, reaching
for her red pen and an index card.

She wrote for a minute.
Then stopped.
"Words are not enough.
You need to learn to feel
when the dough
has just enough flour."

That very afternoon, together,
we measured, stirred
and measured again,
matching the day's humidity
with the correct amount of flour.
After her spoon declared
the mix "correct," she
watched me bring the spoon
round and round the bowl
until I could too "feel" the dough's
message of "thick enough."

We oiled her special press,
laughed, as I burned the first few,
efforts. Two hours later we
proudly set a plate of
finely finished
specimens before my father and my husband.

Only then, Mom wrote out the recipe.
Next, she took me to buy a *pizzelle* iron
from the man who sold one to her.

Around the Round Oak Table

Around the round oak table
revolves our nightly show.
No matter how fast the daily grind,
over dinner, we take it slow.

No masks at this venue.
Entertainment for all.
Set the table,
Pour the water,
Serve the food,
Pray.
Let's Eat!
Curtain's up!
Dinnertime!

Equal billing to food and talk
Freely passed round the table.

Pasta, salad, meat fill plates as we
dish the day's events,
hopes, highs, lows.
  a cacophony of topics—
Simpsons... Buffy...
Death penalty... test scores...
George Washington and golf!

By the time plates are empty, hearts are full.
Long after the sweetness of dessert is a memory,
Words continue to be served up in hearty portions.
Conversation's everyone's favorite course at the round oak table.

In Eliot's rooms *"the women come and go*
Talking of Michaelangleo"
Around the round oak table, love is spoken—loudly, and by all.

Strawberries

Cherokee love fruit.
Strewn by gods on path
of an angry maiden
who stopped her flight to
gather them, anger melting
with each sweet bite,
love for her sweetheart
overcoming her anger.
I think about this as I slice
these heart-shaped treats
into bowls for my dearest.
We argued this morning.

Peach Vendor

A Peach Vendor
takes over the corner at the gas station
at SC57 and 904 on Memorial Day.
Under a blue awning, he lines up
paper bags of orange and red fruit
(at $6 per bag) on an old blue picnic table.
As summer progresses,
wave after wave of
different varieties
fill the bags. Each week I
ask as I hand him six one-dollar bills.
"What's the name of this kind?"
Each week, he shakes
his white-haired head at me,
"It's enough that
they be juicy and sweet."
Out of his jeans pocket,
he pulls a pocketknife.
unfolds it, and with one hand,
slices an entire peach into
tasty little wedges.
The slices lay like petals
in his palm. I pick a slice;
 pop it into my mouth.
As soon as that bit of peach
touches my tongue
it sends shockwaves
of sugar to my brain.
As I murmur, "ummmm"
a driblet of juice escapes my mouth
and races to the edge of my chin.

The man smiles.
With his other hand,
he pockets my six, one-dollar bills.
I pick up my bag
of delicious, though anonymous
peaches. "See you next week,"
we say, saluting each other.
So it goes, each week
until autumn's apples
replace peaches at the stand.

Peaches and Dares

"Do I dare to eat a peach?"—
so asks Eliot.
My smiling sweetheart
brings Carolina peaches to me
in a baskets from the farm market.
We cut and slice
and sample fresh fruit
together.
We cook many into jam and pies
together.
With the scent of peaches
on our hands;
their sweet taste in our mouths,
we dare all this and more—
together.

Two Cups of Coffee

We stopped for a cup of coffee
after crossing the Bosphorus.
We watched the café owner
pour thick sweet coffee
from a copper *cezve*,
into china liners set into matching
brass cup holders.
On retrieving our cups,
he peered into
the remaining swirled
muddy grounds
"I see a trip."
We fulfilled his prophecy
on the ferry to ride back
to Istanbul's European side.

We browsed
Bazaar trinkets,
wandered into
the workers' café where we
lunched on lamb kabobs
at a communal tables with
students and stall salesmen.
One angry young man
pulled out a chair next to me.
He harangued,
"Americans do not like Turkey;
you do not appreciate our culture."
I ordered coffee for the table.
"We love your land," I responded.
My mother nodded, nervously.
We three then chatted back and forth,

across the Bosphorus of our
diverse lives, until his anger waned.
My mother smiled at him.
Upon leaving, I glanced at his empty cup
to scan the future
from his coffee grounds.
Too muddy to read.
I could only hope,
that as our hearts were now more open,
we left him, also, with a softer heart.

Turkish Delight

Bought a box
of Turkish delight
having read of its
delicate deliciousness
in a favorite novel.
One taste revealed all.
A fictional character's delight
can be a reader's
sticky mess.

In Rhapsodic Praise of Biscuits

Biscuits transubstantiate from
buttermilk, Lily brand flour and
Clabber Girl baking powder
into a heavenly delight.
So, it is only right that they
are the first item passed
after pre-prandial prayer.
Plucking one from the basket
passed to me,
my fingers tingle as they brush
the lightly crisp top.
Slowly I separate the still warm
bread of perfection
into two perfect halves,
tamping down the steam
with a pat of real butter
and a swirl of honey.
I lift one section to mouth
and savor the
sweetness of the topping
aided and abetted by the salty,
creamy, butter amid the
biscuit crumbs.
Edible perfection.

If you want to argue,
send me a note.
I will chew it between
two biscuit halves
while reaching for
yet another biscuit.

Fourth of July Picnic, 1955

Before Kennywood
banned bring-in food,
we packed eggplant "parm,"
spaghetti, salads.
No cooking on common use grills
for our family.

After a morning of rides,
we spread out across two picnic tables—
cousins, aunts, uncles,
Grandma, parents—
to eat and talk
and talk and eat
until the long day's sun
burned the sky away.

Darkness brought
fireworks and
running with sparklers
between the picnic tables.

When all lights
and noise gave
way to the quiet
twinkling of night stars,
we piled into assorted Oldsmobiles,
Fords, and Studebakers
and headed home.

The Queen of Long Division

Sometime in my early years
I caught what they called the "Asian flu."
During the three weeks
erased from my schooling
the nuns taught the rest of the class
the intricate secrets of long division.
I never did catch up.
However, my distinct lack of skills
with divisor and dividend
never held me back on Halloween,
where I was the undisputed Queen
of cousinly candy divisions, long and short.

On finishing our separate rounds
of sugary beggary in our
separate neighborhoods,
we seven gathered at Grandma's.
While the grownups talked of
who knows what,
we spilled out our loot
onto her red wool oriental rug.
We stacked our holdings
into categories in front of us like chips—
chocolates, popcorn balls, the nut things,
boxes of jellied chewies,
good and plenty and the rest.
I knew each cousin's favorites
and played one against the other
until the chocolate began to flow my way.
By dividing their interests, I conquered.

I am still shaky with long division,
but when my children
come home with plastic pumpkins full
of chocolate bars, my trading instincts
kick in. My current, hidden stash of candies
attests to the fact that I am still
the Queen of Division, long and otherwise—
when it counts.

Al Dente
> *(Meaning pasta cooked so that it has a slight hardness, "to the tooth," when you bite a strand to determine if it is done)*

We walked into
the new red, white and
green-themed bistro.
"Seat Yourself" a sign
by the register directed.
We did.
A smiling waitress wandered up
to our table as we studied
the chalkboard offering
of pasta-bilities
and other choices
artfully scribbled out
above the bar.
I smiled too and asked
"Is your pasta al dente?"
She sauntered back to the kitchen,
returning a few minutes
later. She reported,
"No Al Dente's ever worked here.
No one in the kitchen
has seen any sign of him."

We ordered pizza.

The Conversation

"My daughter comes and goes," Mom says.
"I am your daughter," I announce.
I stand by her straight green chair
and take her hand in mine.
Her head turns toward me,
but her eyes stare without focus.

Bending toward her, I ask,
"Would you like a drink of water?'
"My daughter comes and goes," she answers.
From her pink plastic pitcher,
I pour the water into a cup.
I pour until I am empty.

I place the cup in her hand,
closing her fingers around it, one by one.
She raises the water to open lips,
but tilts the cup too soon.
She wants to drink,
but cannot find her mouth.

I mop the spill and get more water.
I raise the fresh cup to her lips.
She smiles, sips, and slips her hand over mine.
"My daughter comes and goes," she says.
"My mother too, " I answer,
hug her hard and kiss her.

Dreaming across the Styx

My father walks into my room
wearing his long tan trench coat.
A finely blocked felt hat
tops his jet-black, wavy hair.
He tamps down the tobacco
in his cherry wood pipe, then turns
to me, his brown eyes twinkling.
He steps back into
a poorly lit hallway I do not recognize.
Dad removes his coat and
sits in an orange plastic chair.
Coat on his lap,
he draws softly on the pipe and
nods toward me .
Cherry -flavored tobacco smoke
soothes me.
Dad is waiting for me,
as always.
Through theatre classes
piano lessons, dance lessons.
Patiently enmeshed in his own thoughts,
he waits without complaint.

Suddenly I wake.
I'm at home.
No hallway. No chair.
No cherry tobacco.
Only the smell of coffee.
My father smiles from his photo.
Some say dreaming across the Styx means
Ferryman Charon will soon arrive.

Not for me.

Instead of Charon,
my own beloved father
waits, patiently, to
ferry me across the Styx
in his white 1960 Thunderbird.

A Platter of Mezze

Nightly, I watched this young man
dodging traffic
to cross the street at sunset
while keeping tight hold on
a large platter.
I could set my clock by his,
arrival, when the sun sets.
I guessed he was bringing
Iftar goodies to
friends living in my building.

It became a ritual,
in that time of Ramadan,
just before dusk, in the glow of the moon
to glance out my window
to spot the *mezze* messenger.

One evening I was
in the lobby.
I held the door for him.
He thanked me, smiled, and spoke:
"Please, lift the tray cover,
Take some dates. Try the *katayef*."
I smiled. "No, thank you."
He continued to the elevator
to break fast with his friends.

Not long after
that Ramadan
I moved from that
apartment and forgot
about my smiling friend.

Last night, a photo
of my *mezze* messenger
filled the screen on CNN
and told of a fiery fate,
of the young man, a
Jordanian pilot killed by ISIS.
The announcer spoke his name,
"Moath al-Kasasbeh";
My first thought was,
"Who will bring the *mezze* now?"
If only my tears could quench flames.

Joan Leotta has been playing with words on page and stage since her childhood in Pittsburgh, PA. Her first work published in a national magazine came at age 14—a poem in the Horn Book Magazine. Since then she has followed several career paths, turning to a dual career win writing and story performance as a stay-at-home Mom in the 1980s.

As a writer, Joan is a journalist, novelist, essayist, poet and playwright. Over the years, she has written on parenting, storytelling, and food among other topics, for local newspapers and local and national magazines wherever she has lived. Since moving to North Carolina twelve years ago, she shifted her focus to fiction and poetry. Joan's Italian heritage is evident in the poems in this book and in most of her other writing. Her four historical novels from Desert Breeze publishing, The Legacy of Honor series, feature strong Italian-American women, food and family, during times of war.

Joan's poems and picture books also celebrate food and family. Her poetry and essays appear in or are forthcoming in Gnarled Oak, Red Wolf, A Quiet Courage, the A-3 Review, Hobart Literary Review, Silver Birch, Postcard Poems and Prose among others. She has always considered writing for children as a high calling and in the past two years, THEAQLLC has published four of her picture books: Whoosh!, Summer in a Bowl, Rosa and the Red Apron, and Rosa's Shell.

Joan performs folk tales in schools, museums and festivals for children and adults. Her love for history comes out in performance of two different one-woman shows, one that depicts a strong woman in the Civil War era and another that shows life on the home front during the American Revolution.

Her tagline, "encouraging words through pen and performance" expresses a challenge to herself in her writing and stage work meaning that she wants to inspire the creativity of others with her work. To this end, she often gives classes to help others learn to tap into their creativity to express their thoughts on page and or stage.

When she is not chained to her computer, writing, you can find Joan walking on the beach, in the kitchen working on new recipes, or traveling with her husband, Joe, and daughter, Jennie.

You can reach her with comments, or to request a class or performance, though her blog site at www.joanleotta.wordpress.com and Joan Leotta, Author and Story Performer on Facebook.

www.ingramcontent.com/pod-product-compliance
Lightning Source LLC
LaVergne TN
LVHW041512070426
835507LV00012B/1516